Also by Anthea Peries

Cancer and Chemotherapy

Coping with Cancer & Chemotherapy Treatment: What You Need to Know to Get Through Chemo Sessions

Coping with Cancer: How Can You Help Someone with Cancer, Dealing with Cancer Family Member, Facing Cancer Alone, Dealing with Terminal Cancer Diagnosis, Chemotherapy Treatment & Recovery

Chemotherapy Survival Guide: Coping with Cancer & Chemotherapy Treatment Side Effects

Chemotherapy Chemo Side Effects And The Holistic Approach: Alternative, Complementary And Supplementary Proven Treatments Guide For Cancer Patients

Chemotherapy Treatment: Comforting Gift Book For Patients Coping With Cancer

Christian Books

Seeking Salvation, Secure In Belief: How To Get Sure-Fire Saved By Grace Through Faith, Rapture Ready And Heaven Bound

Thriving In Chaos: A Practical Guide To Surviving In A World Of Uncertainty: Strategies and Tools for Building Resilience, Finding Stability, and Flourishing in Turbulent Times

Divine Mathematics: Unveiling the Secrets of Gematria Exploring the Mystical & Symbolic Significance of Numerology in Jewish and Christian Traditions, & Beyond

The Divine Library: A Short Comprehensive Summary Guide to the Bible: From Genesis to Revelation, Discover the Power, Purpose and Meaning of Scripture in the World's Most Influential Book

Daughters of Faith: The Untold Stories of Women of Power and Strength in the Bible| Rediscovering the Courage, Resilience, Belief And Trust of Females In Scripture

Paul The Apostle Of Christ: From Persecutor To Preacher Exploring the Life, Ministry, and Legacy of A Man Who Transformed Christianity, Spreading the Gospel Across the Mediterranean

Mastering Your Money: A Practical Guide to Budgeting and Saving For Christians Take Control of Your Finances and Achieve Your Financial Goals with 10 Simple Steps

Colon and Rectal

Bowel Cancer Screening: A Practical Guidebook For FIT (FOBT) Test, Colonoscopy & Endoscopic Resection Of Polyp Removal In The Colon

Cancer: Bowel Screening| A Simple Guide About How It Works To Help You Decide

Eating Disorders

Food Cravings: Simple Strategies to Help Deal with Craving for Sugar & Junk Food

Sugar Cravings: How to Stop Sugar Addiction & Lose Weight

The Immune System, Autoimmune Diseases & Inflammatory Conditions: Improve Immunity, Eating Disorders & Eating for Health

Food Addiction: Overcome Sugar Bingeing, Overeating on Junk Food & Night Eating Syndrome

Food Addiction: Overcoming your Addiction to Sugar, Junk Food, and Binge Eating

Food Addiction: Why You Eat to Fall Asleep and How to Overcome Night Eating Syndrome

Overcome Food Addiction: How to Overcome Food Addiction, Binge Eating and Food Cravings

Emotional Eating: Stop Emotional Eating & Develop Intuitive Eating Habits to Keep Your Weight Down

Emotional Eating: Overcoming Emotional Eating, Food Addiction and Binge Eating for Good

Eating At Night Time: Sleep Disorders, Health and Hunger Pangs: Tips On What You Can Do About It

Addiction To Food: Proven Help For Overcoming Binge Eating Compulsion And Dependence

Weight Loss: How To Not Gain Holiday Weight After Thanks Giving & Christmas Holidays Beat Post Vacation

Weight Gain: Proven Ways To Jumpstart Healthy Eating

Weight Loss After Having A Baby: How To Lose Postpartum Weight After Pregnancy & Giving Birth

Food Addiction And Emotional Eating Guidebook: Proven Ways To End Binge Eating, Sugar Cravings & Eating At Night-Time

Eating Disorders: Food Addiction & Its Effects, What Can You Do If You Can't Stop Overeating?

Slim Down Sensibly: A Realistic Guide to Achieving
Sustainable Weight Loss A Science-Based Approach to
Healthy Eating, Exercise, and Mindset for Lasting Results

Eye Care
Glaucoma Signs And Symptoms

Food Addiction
Overcoming Food Addiction to Sugar, Junk Food. Stop Binge
Eating and Bad Emotional Eating Habits
Food Addiction: Overcoming Emotional Eating, Binge
Eating and Night Eating Syndrome
Weight Loss Without Dieting: 21 Easy Ways To Lose Weight
Naturally
Weight Loss Affirmations For Food Addicts: You Can Do It
Believe In Yourself Daily Positive Affirmations To Help You
Lose Weight

Grief, Bereavement, Death, Loss
Coping with Loss & Dealing with Grief: Surviving
Bereavement, Healing & Recovery After the Death of a Loved
One
How to Plan a Funeral
Coping With Grief And Heartache Of Losing A Pet: Loss Of
A Beloved Furry Companion: Easing The Pain For Those
Affected By Animal Bereavement

Grieving The Loss Of Your Baby: Coping With The Devastation Shock And Heartbreak Of Losing A Child Through Miscarriage, Still Birth

Loss And Grief: Treatment And Discovery Understanding Bereavement, Moving On From Heartbreak And Despair To Recovery

Grief: The Grieving Process, Reactions, Stages Of Grief, Risks, Other Losses And Recovery

First Steps In The Process Of Dealing With Grief: Help for Grieving People: A Guidebook for Coping with Loss. Pain, Heartbreak and Sadness That Won't Go Away

Health Fitness

How To Avoid Colds and Flu Everyday Tips to Prevent or Lessen The Impact of Viruses During Winter Season

Boost Your Immune System Fast: Guide On Proven Ways For Boosting Your Immunity Against Illness And Disease.

International Cooking

Spicy Seafood Dishes: Gourmet Cooking Ideas For Curry And Spice Lovers. Introductory Guide To Decadent Seafood Cuisine With Health Benefits & Wellbeing For The Connoisseur

Noodles: Noodle Recipes Introductory Guide To Delicious Spicy Cuisine International Asian Cooking

A Taste Of Malaysia: Authentic Recipes For Nasi Lemak, Satay, Laksa, And More: Unveiling The Secrets Of Malaysian Cuisine Through Delicious And Easy-to-Follow Dishes Discovering the Flavours and Traditions of Burma (Myanmar): A Guide to Burmese Cuisine and Culture A Journey Through Food, Fashion, Art and History

Parenting

Anger Management For Stressed-Out Parents:Skills To Help You Cope Better With Your Child

Coding Programs For Kids: Parents Guidebook: How Your Child Can Learn To Code And The Benefits For Their Future

Compassionate Collaborative Communication: How To Communicate Peacefully In A Nonviolent Way A Practical Guide Using Effective Proven Skills For Conflict In Relationships Between Parents & Kids

Potty Training: Handbook Guide In Crap Parenting Proven Ways To Train Your Toddler Easily & Quickly With Realistic Results

Acts Of Kindness: Doing Good Deeds to Help Others

Personal Relationships

How To Talk To Your Partner: Preventing Problems Through Effective Communication In A Relationship

Quark Cheese

50 More Ways to Use Quark Low-fat Soft Cheese: The Natural Alternative When Cooking Classic Meals

Quark Cheese Recipes: 21 Delicious Breakfast Smoothie Ideas Using Quark Cheese

30 Healthy Ways to Use Quark Low-fat Soft Cheese

Introduction To Quark Cheese And 25 Recipe Suggestions: Quark Cheese Guide And Recipes

Quit Alcohol

How To Stop Drinking Alcohol: Coping With Alcoholism, Signs, Symptoms, Proven Treatment And Recovery

Relationships

The Grief Of Getting Over A Relationship Breakup: How To Accept Breaking Up With Your Ex | Advice And Tips To Move On

Coping With A Marriage Breakup: How To Get Over The Emotional Heartbreak Of A Relationship Breakdown, Signs Of Splitting Up, Divorce And Heal From A Broken Heart

Self Help

OCD: Introduction Guide Book Obsessive Compulsive Disorder And How To Recover

Sleep Disorders
Sleep Better at Night and Cure Insomnia Especially When Stressed

Standalone
Family Style Asian Cookbook: Authentic Eurasian Recipes: Traditional Anglo-Burmese & Anglo-Indian
Coping with Loss and Dealing with Grief: The Stages of Grief and 20 Simple Ways on How to Get Through the Bad Days
Coping With Grief Of A Loved One After A Suicide: Grieving The Devastation And Loss Of Someone Who Took Their Own Life. How Long Does The Heartache Last?
When A Person Goes Missing And Cannot Be Found: Coping With The Grief And Devastation, Without Losing Hope, Of When An Adult Or Child Disappears
Menopause For Women: Signs Symptoms And Treatments A Simple Guide
Remembering Me: Discover Your Memory Proven Ways To Expand & Increase It As You Get Older
Boredom: How To Overcome Feeling Bored Discover Over 100 Proven Ways To Beat Apathy
Putting Baby To Sleep: Soothe Your Newborn Baby To Sleep For Longer Stretches At Night Proven Practical Survival Guide For Tired Busy New Parents
Coping With Bullying And Cyberbullying: What Parents, Teachers, Office Managers, And Spouses Need To Know:

How To Identify, Deal With And Cope With A Bully At Home, In School Or In The Workplace

Gardening For Beginners: How To Improve Mental Health, Happiness And Well Being Outdoors In The Garden: Green Finger Holistic Approach In Nature: Everything You Need To Know, Even If You Know Nothing!

Becoming Vegan For Health And The Environment: Plant Based Veganism Guidebook For Beginners: Balanced View Of The Benefits & Risks Of Being Vegetarian

Happiness & Reading Books: For Adults & Children A Proven Way To Increase Literacy Focus Improve Memory Sleep Better Relieve Stress Broaden Your Knowledge Increase Confidence Motivation & Be Happy

Caring For A Loved One With Cancer & Chemotherapy Treatment: An Easy Guide for Caregivers

Genealogy Tracing Your Roots A Comprehensive Guide To Family History Research Uncovering Your Ancestry, Building Your Family Tree And Preserving Your Heritage

Table of Contents

SEEKING SALVATION, SECURE IN BELIEF

How To Get Sure-Fire Saved By Grace Through Faith, Rapture Ready And Heaven Bound

Anthea Peries

Disclaimer: This book is not intended as a substitute for God's written Word in the Bible but as an aid in studying the Bible and getting saved according to Paul's good news Gospel in the New Testament.

Introduction

———

Why do we feel depressed, and why are we in troubled end times right now? Why does this world feel so different?

Do you sense something is about to happen?

Are you a baby Christian wishing to know more about Jesus Christ right now?

It can appear a little confusing, right? There is so much information out there, and doctrines are being mingled and muddled.

Do you want to know how you can get saved?

Or you know someone that needs to be?

Perhaps you are not a Christian and want to know more?

Whoever you are, I am glad that you purchased this book to find out more.

We are all sinners, and as we get older, we are going to die. It is what it is. Jesus Christ died for our sins and rose from the dead for us. We don't need to be depressed or in despair, and prayers can help lift us and give hope. Since God is merciful, he will forgive us if we ask Him to forgive us of our sins.

But why do we feel so depressed?

Because we have sinned in our lives and deserve hell.

Why are we in troubled end times?

Because Jesus Christ is coming back soon, and we need to be ready to meet him.

We have fallen short, and we are going to hell unless we accept Jesus' free gift. We believe in who he is, asking Jesus into our lives.

The Bible says in John 3,17 that anyone who hates his brother or sister is a murderer and has committed the perfect sin.

The Bible says in Revelation 21:8-10 that everyone who has not been beheaded for the Gospel of God will be saved. Also, it says in Revelation 20:15 And if anyone's name was not found written in the book of life, he was thrown into the lake of fire.

Sense Of Belonging

———

Have you been searching for your real home? Have you felt like you don't belong here anymore? What is this calling that you feel?

It seems to be the Lord, but how can that be when we only believe in part of the Bible, and he tells us not to. It is confusing, and we get so frustrated with our thoughts and life. What is this calling, and why have we been searching for it all our life? We are afraid for our life. It seems to be real. What should I do?

Some believe that the Lord is not here with us on earth, and he must be on another level of heaven or somewhere else. He has returned to his Father, and that is where he will be forever. But he gave the Holy Spirit to dwell in each of us who believes in him, our comforter and guide.

Some people are not Christian. Yet, they feel they are closer to God than most Christians. I look at the world as it is, and it feels that the Lord has left for good. And from all that he says in the Bible, he has returned to his Father. But with the presence of the Holy Spirit in each of us who believe in him and who are saved, we know that God never lies and that Jesus is coming back very soon to take his bride, the Church, out of here.

How Do We Find God?

———

Many people are searching for answers to many of these questions:

Let us start with what is the definition of God?

What does it mean to find God and his kingdom in heaven, not on earth?

How do we build a relationship with God?

Is there a difference between Jesus Christ and the Holy Spirit?

Do you know how to tell if someone is saved or not saved?

Do you know why Paul preached Christianity and evangelism, telling the good news about Jesus Christ to others *Who may not have heard it?*

What does it mean to be saved?

What does the Bible say about end times Bible prophesy?

Being Like Jesus Christ In Troubled Times

———

H ow can we evangelise to help spread Paul's Gospel of salvation to Christians and non-Christians living near us, as well as across the world?

How can we join forces with other Christians worldwide and help end the world's suffering as we work together for the sake of our Lord Jesus Christ?

A Christian who is in a place where they don't know how to search for God deceives themselves. This is harmful to their walk with God. This is how their sins will get revealed after they die. Searching for God should be done from the heart, not by searching on the internet or books. To find God, you need to be spiritually hungry and thirsty for him. You also need to have an honest heart, asking Him what to do.

Like the two disciples on their way to Emmaus, they met Jesus Christ and had Him explain the scriptures to them. He opened up their minds to understand, and "*their eyes were opened*" So they could see the truth about what was written in the Old Testament.

Don't allow yourself to become spiritually deceived. Don't let others deceive you, either. There is only one way to heaven, and that is through Jesus Christ, our Lord. There are no other ways except blasphemy. This false way of trying to find God is sinful. God never gave his Son to those who believe that there are different ways besides believing in Jesus Christ to get saved because he said he was *the only way*.

The Lord, our God, will deal with those who go against his Word. There is only one way to heaven, and that is through Jesus Christ, our Lord. The Bible tells us in the book of John 5:24 that "*He who rejects me rejects him who sent me.*"

God's justice reveals how to find God. "Heaven" is for real, and it exists. It is not just a state of mind but a place in the clouds or somewhere else. "Heaven" is the place where people live with God and reign with him. In a state of mind where they are no longer in a sinful state but transformed in his perfect, holy character. Living with God is a relationship that they have had to abide by and not one that can be done overnight or at the moment of death.

We know what heaven is like; we see it every day when we pray to our Father in Heaven. When we read the stories found in the New Testament of Jesus Christ and his closest disciples living with God for all eternity, we see it as their neighbours.

We believe, but others have seen it with our own eyes! The apostle John wrote about heaven being an actual place or space. (John 14:2, 3. 1 Corinthians 15:40-42)

The angel Gabriel told Mary that she would "*conceive and give birth to a son who is his Lord [Jesus]*". (Luke 1:34)

And we know that this is true because of what we see in the New Testament. But Mary did not understand that this means that she would have a relationship with God, which was God's plan for her. (Luke 1:36) She understood it as her "*being with a man*" who would have children, which was Joseph's plan for her in the fleshly sense. (Luke 1:34)

She didn't understand it until "*the angel Gabriel was sent from God to [her]",* telling her that what she was going to have would be the Son of God. (Luke 1:35) It is here where Gabriel told Mary about God, His plan for her, and the roles she, Joseph, and Jesus Christ would have in it all.

There is a real place away from this world called "heaven",; an actual place wherein God is our ruler and guide in place of Satan (the prince of this world).

We are in a perfect, peaceful environment with our deceased loved ones in this place or state. We have no sickness, pain, or sorrows to grieve because Jesus Christ is our refuge. The New Testament gives us an example of heaven in the book of Revelation by John the Revelator. (Revelation 21:2)

There is a period when those called and chosen before the earth's foundation will claim their inheritance as heirs to heaven. Those who live in the flesh will inherit the earth.

As heirs of heaven, they will live lives here on earth as servants to heaven. The law of inheritance given to the saints in the book of Revelation chapter 22:12-17.

But I say unto you, That whosoever looketh on a woman to lust after her hath committed adultery with her already in his heart. (Matthew 5:28)

You have heard that it was said to those of old, "*Thou shalt not commit adultery.*" But I say to you that whoever looks at a woman to lust for her has already committed adultery with her in his heart. (Matthew 5:27-28).

Many people believe that the Bible is true because it conflicts with what they see with their eyes and feel with their hands. God knows our sinful nature, and so He hides His truth behind a veil called the *mystery*. (2nd Corinthians 3:13, Romans 16:25,26.).

This means that God holds back some of His truth from us until the time. He has appointed for them to be revealed to us. (John 15:15)

We know from some of the passages in the Bible on spiritual gifts that God can do both at the same time and for all eternity as we look upon Him face to face. (Romans 12:6, 1st Corinthians 13:12).

And I heard a loud voice from the throne saying, "Behold, the tabernacle of God is among men, and He shall dwell among them, and they shall be His people, and God Himself shall be among them." (Revelation 21:3)

When God gave the inheritance to Israel, he gave it to an entire nation as a family-owned estate. This was because they were the chosen people of God to be His firstborn Son. (Exodus 4:22, Hosea 11:1). The entire nation was given an inheritance so that it could be spread out over all of them.

(Genesis 12:2, Genesis 15:1-6, Genesis 15:18-21, Genesis 17:4) This is one reason God gave a double portion to the Son of Jacob, Joseph, in Egypt. (Genesis 45:8). This means that it would be divided into two parts or halves by a river or stream, or it could mean that it would be surrounded by water on all sides like an island. This can also be understood by what God did with Joseph. (Genesis 41:41-43). God took Joseph to a safe place. He protected him from enemies and gave him food and water. God made sure that no harm would come to him. This was so that he would be safe from any danger. Another part of this family would not survive until the end of their lives. The other family members had different problems from those of the first Son. He was given an inheritance because they were given an inheritance by promise rather than by birthright. (Deuteronomy 27:63).

The Birthright Blessing was the combination of both the 12 tribes of Israel and Judah, which became the nation of Israel.

14

Get Saved According To The New Testament Paul's Gospel

———

How do you find God?

What is the closest you can be to God? How do you become closer to him?

How do you get more in touch with him and build a relationship with him?

There are many ways, but there is one easy way. To become closer to God, you don't need any special privilege or spiritual achievements. It's just a simple matter of listening carefully. You can come closer to God if you listen carefully. The Bible says, *"if you abide in my word, then are you, my disciples, indeed, and you shall know the truth*." John 8:31-32.

If you listen to God's Word, he will speak to your heart and mind. You can be in touch with him through his words, his love letter to us, the Bible. Then he will speak to your heart, and he will say, "I love you". Not just a polite nice, but a love which wants you to be close to him; and wants to be close to you. God's love is not something we can fully understand with our mind, but we can feel his love with our hearts. Listening carefully means reading God's Word and the Bible and understanding what he wants you to do. He doesn't want you to go here or there. He gives you clear directions on how to live your life through his words. It's up to us whether we listen

15

carefully or not. The truth is that God's Word is the easiest way to get to know him.

However, if you just follow his words and do not go out of your way to do something for God, he will let you know. He will send you signs and miracles to message that it's not the right time to do certain things for him. He will let you know that it is not the right time for you.

You may go through trials and tribulations or receive some kind of tragedy, hardship or disappointment. Still, God will remain close with you through it all. "For my thoughts are not your thoughts, nor are your ways my ways, declares the LORD." Isaiah 55:8.

God wants us to listen carefully first, then do something for him when we hear his Word and understand His Will. We try to understand what he wants from us and go out of our way to do it for him, rather than just going on with our daily lives without giving God any thought.

He will let us know that he is more than happy to be close with us. He will send us his miracles and blessings. His miracles and blessings are the closest we can be to him. He is willing to do that for you if you listen carefully and then do what he wants from you when you understand his Will.

God is trying to communicate with us through his Word, the Bible. Suppose we open our hearts and minds to receive his message. Our minds may be full of images from the T.V. or the internet or our worries, busy lives etc., that God's words can't get in.

He tells us how to live our lives, but our worries and busy lives keep us from listening to him. We read his Word, but we don't understand what he is trying to tell us.

We need time for God each day to listen attentively to his words. He will tell you what he wants you to do through his Word, but if you are too busy with your worries or your everyday activities, you can't hear him because your mind is full of other things.

Think of it this way; it's like a radio: when it's not turned on, no sound comes through it. If the radio is turned on, but there is nothing on the station, no sound will come through it. You may have the volume on high, but still, you won't hear anything because the radio is not picking up any signals.

It's a kind of living called "living in the flesh". The flesh is our body and soul and the emotions from which we think and feel. The Bible tells us that we are to live in the Spirit, not in the flesh. People who live in the flesh live their lives caring only about themselves and their thoughts, feelings and situations.

They are far too busy with their feelings or their cares or worries to be able to think about God. Or listen carefully to his Word as he communicates with us through it. They tend to be noisy and busy with their thoughts or feelings, so they don't hear God's voice.

When we learn to follow the way that God has given us to live, our mind will be quiet. Our mind will not be full of what we think or feel but will have God's Word from the Bible in it.

Then God will speak to our heart, and our heart will want us to do what he wants us to do.

How Often Should We And Study The Bible?

———

Do we believe the Bible is the Word of God? Our understanding of salvation and eternal life is undoubtedly essential, but how we read and interpret Scripture matters even more, especially in the correct doctrine and dispensation.

God reveals His truth through His Word, NOT through our interpretation of it. The Bible can be problematic in that humans have misinterpreted it throughout history. Some interpretations are more accurate than others, but it is impossible to make up an interpretation that has always been true.

Some criticise and attack their Bibles, saying it's wrong, missing things. But should we all read and study the Bible in unison and get on the same page?

Do we believe the Bible is the Word of God?

As said before, our understanding of salvation and eternal life is undoubtedly essential, but how we read and interpret Scripture matters even more.

The Bible cannot be considered a human-invented storybook or fairy tale. It is a divine revelation to mankind from God (1 Timothy 3:16-17). It is the infallible, inspired Word of God

(2 Timothy 3:16-17). Because it purports to be from God, we know that it is true.

God does not contradict Himself but rather reveals Himself in His Word. As Christians, we claim that the Bible is the only infallible source of knowledge about God (Isaiah 8:20; Acts 17:11; Romans 15:4; 2 Timothy 3:15).

It is the only model for our spiritual life (1 Peter 1:23-25).

It is the only authority (John 3:33; 3:19; 1 Corinthians 8:1; 2 Timothy 1:13; Hebrews 4:12).

In short, God's Word is our sole basis for believing everything else that is true and of value.

However, some think that the Bible contains errors because it claims to be God's Word. Only because numerous passages have been mistranslated, misinterpreted, or omitted altogether through time and translation. As a result, some passages are problematic for us to understand today (the book of Revelation is one example). Moreover, there are numerous additions and subtractions in our Bibles (2 Peter 3:16-17).

God surely did not inspire erroneous or incomplete communications.

When we read passages in the Bible that do not seem to make sense to us or are difficult for us to believe, we tend to fix the problem by changing our interpretation. As a result, we have changed our understanding of God over time.

Today, most Christians would probably be uncomfortable with the incarnation and resurrection of Jesus if they had lived during His period or even the first century.

Although the Bible speaks with clarity about God's love and grace, we must also read it in harmony with other sources. The New Testament affirms that we should not accept all things as literally true but rather interpret them figuratively (John 3:15-16). We must also be careful to use good hermeneutical methods (including interlinear study); church tradition, and overall reason when reading the Bible (1 Corinthians 14:30; 1 Peter 1:24).

Anyone who reads and understands Scripture correctly will come to the same conclusion. However, suppose we allow our minds to be changed or our understanding of God's Word is wrong. In that case, we are following a bad philosophy as a result of faulty methods.

Our Errors In Interpreting Scripture

Why do we have different ways of interpreting the Bible?

Why does it sometimes seem as if our interpretations describe completely different gods?

And how can some Christians believe that we are all saved and destined for the same eternal life when they read so many conflicting passages in the Bible?

Although there is one God and one salvation, there are many ways to get to Heaven (Romans 1:20). The human mind in itself is not capable of understanding all of God's truth with absolute clarity. But with the help of the Holy Spirit, we can understand more than ever (1 Corinthians 2:14-16).

When we read specific passages in the Bible, our minds are capable of being deceived and confused. Traditional interpretations can be incorrect, even if they have been around for thousands of years. Outdated translations can be misleading.

Because the Bible is a human book, it contains human language and human errors (John 10:35). And although God's love is a guiding principle in His Word, it is not always expressed as it should (Matthew 5:43-48; 1 Corinthians 13:1-13).

The only way we can understand God's truth is to understand that the Bible focuses on the Jews and Gentiles in different ways at various points in time. And, of course, what we should do in this life to achieve eternity with Him.

The New Testament writings by Paul was written for the Gentiles. His writings tell us that we must repent, place our faith in Jesus and be baptised into Him by the Holy Spirit. We must deny sin, forsake the world and pursue righteousness.

The old law was fulfilled in Christ (Matthew 5:17-18; Romans 6:14). **We are not saved by our good works or religious rituals under the old law but by faith through grace alone** (Ephesians 2:8-9).

Because of these shortfalls, we can become confused about what the Bible says. There are places where it seems as if God is contradicting Himself (such as the issue of divorce and remarriage; 1 Corinthians 7:10-11 vs Matthew 5:31-32).

Some of God's commandments can be difficult for us to obey, such as loving our enemies and praying for those who persecute us (Matthew 5:43-48; Luke 6:27-28).

We may even be tempted not to read the Scripture because we may think we can't live up to what it says. But at the same time, we need God's grace and mercy more than ever.

Many times, God's words seem harsh and harmful. The Bible teaches that He allows sicknesses and accidents to chasten us. Even though it is not always obvious how His wrath will result in good for those who are righteous (Job 13:24-25; James 1:3).

God's ways are not our ways (Isaiah 55:8-9). But we still serve a God of love, who sent His only begotten Son to suffer and die for us, for our sins. We need to have a right view of God and accept our human frailty. Our lives are totally in His hands

(Matthew 10:29-31; Job 1:21; Psalm 22:27; John 19:30). He will never leave us, nor forsake us (Hebrews 13:5).

God does not change with time, culture or situation.

Throughout history, God has demonstrated the same unchanging character (Malachi 3:6). But people can change, depending on whether they are aligned with Him or against Him. This is His plan (Isaiah 48:10). We should be thankful to the God who turned the hardness of our hearts to compassion and who wept at the death of Jesus Christ.

We need to ask for His grace. He wants to give it to us with our permission. God wants everyone to get saved by his Son Jesus Christ; he is the only way!

God's Plan For Your Life

———

D

o not ever be afraid. Pray and seek God's help in reading through this book so that you will have the right view of Him and can apply what you learn in your life.

- *See Psalms 106:13; 126:1-3; Isaiah 12:2-4; 60:14-21; 63:7-8; James 1:19; Revelation 1:17.*
- *See Isaiah 53, 54; Daniel 9:4-18; Jeremiah 16:19.*
- *See Exodus 34:6-7; John 3:16; Romans 4:20-21.*
- *See John 3:36.*
- *See Genesis 15:1,8,9; 18:18-19; Joel 2:32.*
- *See Matthew 26:34-35.*
- *See Luke 2:25,38; John 4:13-14,30,31; Acts 5, 7.*

An Overview Of The Bible

———

W hat is the Bible?
Who wrote it?

How was it written?

What does the Bible contain?

What is the Bible not?

These are all excellent questions to consider as well. Very briefly, before we dig in further, here's a brief overview of what an English Bible looks like:

And there appeared a great wonder in heaven; a woman clothed with the sun, and the moon under her feet, and upon her head a crown of twelve stars:

And she being with child cried, travailing in birth, and pained to be delivered. When her water broke forthwith, she suffered pain and when she might be delivered.

God delivered her that the travailing pains of labour might be accomplished. She brought forth her firstborn, wrapped him in swaddling clothes, and laid him in a manger; because there was no room for them in the inn.

Overview of the Bible.

The word "Bible" comes from the Greek word "biblos," which means "books."

In 539 B.C., the Hebrew Royal Court ordered all of the texts of the Hebrew Bible to be collected into one bound volume (the Torah or Five Books of Moses).

And it was presented to King Josiah. As a result, that Hebrew Bible was named the "Bible."

In What Language Was The Bible Written?

The Old Testament was originally written primarily in Hebrew. The New Testament (the Gospel of Jesus Christ) was written in Greek by men and women who knew very little Hebrew. They wrote in the Koine Greek dialect or common Greek of that day.

The Books Of The Bible

———

The first 39 books are known as the Old Testament and were arranged from longest to shortest. They were all written by Jews living in the Land of Israel, but there were no chapters, no verses. They are arranged in order of authors from Moses to Malachi and are subdivided into verses or paragraphs.

The book of Esther written in the book of Ezra and Esther. Each book has its author (who also wrote most, if not all, of the other books), and they didn't start numbering their books until around 250 B.C.

Authority To Write The Bible

———

The 24 elders wrote down all that came out of the mouth of God (Old Testament). Jesus said, "*No one knows the Son except the Father, and no one knows the Father except the Son and anyone to whom the Son chooses to reveal him*" (Matthew 11:27).

The apostles who spoke with Christ worked alongside him in creating and spreading his Gospel (the New Testament). God taught them, and when they wrote the words that Jesus Christ himself quoted. They wrote what God wanted them to write.

There is not one error in any book in the Bible. It is an accurate historical record of all that happened in both testaments and everything that Jesus Christ foretold.

Who Decided Which Books Belong In The Bible?

―――

"The Apocrypha," a group of books not included in over 95% of the world's bibles, was never included in the Hebrew Bible. The Old Testament divided into three parts:

1. *The Law (Torah, first five books),*
2. *The Prophets*
3. *Writings.*

The law comprises the first five books, **Genesis, Exodus, Leviticus, Numbers and Deuteronomy**.

The Prophets made up of *Isaiah, Jeremiah, Lamentations, Ezekiel* and the twelve minor prophets: *Hosea, Joel, Amos and Obadiah.*

The early Church chose only those writings that agreed with their beliefs.

These writings or books have been carefully preserved and are now called the **New Testament**.

The early Church never accepted the other writings that made up the Apocrypha because they conflicted with what God had already told us in his Word.

What is the Bible not?

The Bible is *not a science text*; it is not an encyclopaedia.

The Bible is not a history book.

It is a religious text. If you want to know the history of the world, there are plenty of texts available.

The Bible is not a novel.

Some stories written by authors had visions and dreams from God and recorded as such.

Difference Between The Old Testament And New Testament

———

They are two separate testaments representing **two entirely different covenants** that God made with a man (to keep his commandments).

God made one covenant with the Jewish people and one covenant for all Christians.

1. God made one covenant with the Jewish people who lived in Jerusalem during Moses' time (The Old Testament)
2. and the second covenant with all gentiles, Christians (Jews first) who believe in Jesus Christ as their Lord and Saviour (the New Testament).

The O.T. teaches the Old Testament Laws, and the N.T. teaches New Testament Laws.

How many books are in the Bible?

Thirty-nine books in the Old Testament covers 600 years of history (from creation to Moses).

There are *27 books in the New Testament* covering 2000+ years of Christian history. The short answer: there are over 41,000 words in the Bible.

There are over 100 chapters and over 40,000 verses in each book. The total Bible has a word count of 138 billion words. And 679 pages just for footnotes!

Dispensationalism

———

Dispensationalism is a way of dividing the Word of God. Under Webster's 1828 dictionary, dispensation refers to administering various matters to diverse groups of people.

Dispensationalism is the theory that different times in God's history plan are divided into "dispensations" or periods. God initially deals with a man more directly. For example, a dispensation may be from about 600 B.C. to A.D. 70 (the time just before Jesus was born).

Historically, dispensationalism is a Protestant doctrine that has gained prominence among some modern charismatics. It is most often associated with John Nelson Darby (1800-1882), who first developed the doctrine in his book, The Seven Dispensations of Daniel. Dispensationalism aims to explain the differences between the Old and New Testaments by using a world-systems model.

Some believe that dispensationalists see a distinction between God's grace and love and Christ's redemptive work in defeating Satan on the cross. Thus, the dividing point between two "dispensations."

For example, God's "dispensation" to Adam seems to be one of protection and blessing for us. Then came Noah, a dispensation of new beginnings, symbolised by the ark that bore Noah and his family through a flood. After the flood came Abraham, a dispensation of government and promise. A dispensation is seen as something that begins with an act of God and ends with an act or a revelation by God.

Dispensationalism has undergone several recent shifts in theology since its most famous proponent, John Nelson Darby (1800-1882), first formulated it in the 19th century. At first, it was a Christian response to criticism from secularists and others who questioned biblical authority.

It was an attempt to present the "Kingdom of God" as being on earth, not in heaven.

In the 1900s, many groups came out against this type of thinking from within Christianity's ranks. This gave dispensationalism a bad reputation. People began to associate it with fundamentalism and even with exclusivism related to certain Pentecostal groups. Some say that there is no room left for "non-dispensationalists" because accepting Christ's second coming means that you must believe in end-times doctrines.

In 1931, dispensationalists changed the name of their movement from "dispensationalism" to "pre-millennialism". This was to distance themselves from fundamentalism and gain acceptance as a more respectable branch of Christianity. Theologically speaking, this proposed shift was quite radical. It put them in direct opposition to historic or non-dispensational pre-millennialism.

Proponents of pre-millennialism traditionally believed that Jesus Christ returned to earth before the millennium (the thousand years mentioned in Revelation 20). They saw this as the same time when Satan would be bound, and Christ would reign on earth for a thousand years.

In the 1970s, dispensationalists shifted their beliefs once again. This time, they moved away from the view that Christ would return before the millennium (1,000 years of peace and righteousness).

Believing that there will be two comings of Jesus into the world (Christ's first coming). Where he died on the cross for our sins as described in 1 Corinthians 15:3-8. And his second coming.

These dispensationalists now saw a period after Christ's second coming in which anti-Christ rule would be established on earth by a coalition of forces headed up by Satan himself. It is believed that Satan will rule the earth in the form of a man until Jesus Christ returns at the end of this Time of Trouble. There is a strong emphasis on developing this belief within its Biblical framework and language. Mainly through dispensationalism's main proponent, Johnathan Cahn, as expressed in his recent book The Harbinger.

Darby himself wrote: "There are two ways of looking at Scripture - one or other is necessary either to embrace a system or reject it altogether."

Darby's formula has proven effective for many individuals who have used it as a way to understand God's Word. Others have found his dispensational system to be too rigid and therefore not helpful to their understanding.

Pastor Gene Kim explains dispensationalism. YouTube video:

https://bit.ly/2RC3fTm

Dispensational Facts

———

Creation of Adam

Salvation is by works alone.

Conscience: Noah and Abraham.

Salvation is by faith and dependant on works, under conscience.

Abraham is the father of physical Israel, and God's covenant with the nation of Israel is everlasting. God will never break (His) covenant with (the Jews), Judges 2:1.

Physical and Spiritual Dealings

The foundation of God's dealings, mainly physical in the Old Testament. But he did deal with people also spiritually; for example, Abraham, in his belief, in the Lord, "*counted him for righteousness.*" Genesis 15:5-6. Yet Abraham's salvation by works later took place years later when he was ready to sacrifice Isaac, James 2. Hence it is essential to divide the times in a dispensational way; there is then no contradiction.

The Law – Moses and David

During Moses' Law, the Jews had to follow the Law of Moses. The Old Testament Jews and Moses' salvation was by faith and works.

Today, we Christians believe that we cannot lose the Holy Spirit even if they fail in our works.

Therefore, the doctrine meant for different groups of people in various periods.

Signs and Wonders

God physically dealt with physical Jews with powerful signs and wonders through Moses.

The Mosaic Law and Christians

We, as Christians today, have Jesus' sacrifice on the cross.

Water Baptism and Works

John the Baptist came, water baptism and works repentance were both involved for salvation (Matthew 3:1-12).

The Kingdom of Heaven

The Kingdom of Heaven is a physical kingdom. Works are involved for salvation in this kingdom. Before Jesus was crucified, he did not preach the Gospel of Christ.

The Kingdom of God

The spiritual kingdom of God is *within* you as a Christian. (Luke 17:21). It is different, unlike the physical kingdom of heaven; it cannot go inside you! This proves it is different.

End Times

Matthew 24 deals with Jewish matters; works for salvation and *post-tribulation Rapture* (Matthew 24:29-31). This Rapture will be for the Jews, not the spiritual Christian. The Church gets raptured before the seven-year tribulation, before the wrath of God upon the Jews.

Christians are not appointed to the wrath of God.

Transitioning from Physical to Spiritual Dealings

Physical Israel was going to reject Jesus. Therefore, God turned towards the Church. Jesus has the authority to bring in spiritual doctrines.

Spiritual dealings are beginning to form in Jesus' time. In Matthew to John, both spiritual Christian doctrines and Jewish doctrines appear. The latter when God was dealing with the Jews.

Works for Salvation

The book of James contains minor amounts of Christian doctrine; he mostly dedicates his writings "*to the twelve tribes which are scattered abroad*". He mentions end-times, the Jew's plan as Jesus said during His ministry, faith and works. James writes "*Ye see then how that by works a man is justified, and not by faith only*" (James2:24).

Physical Signs for Salvation for Jews

- *Water baptism*
- *Healing signs*
- *Physical actions*

Signs and speaking in tongues are for the physical Jews and come from the transitional book, Acts. (Acts 2:4-5). Also referred to as "Jerusalem Jews".

The Apostle Spiritual Dealings

The Apostles agree that salvation is by faith alone without works. They "*gave no such commandment*" regarding circumcision and the law. (Acts 15: 11, 23-24). Salvation involves both faith and works only for Jews in the end-times.

An Apostle, Philip in Acts 8:36-38, taught Christian doctrine. Also, John in 3 John 6, the Church is mentioned.

1 Peter 1:4-5,) also contains Christian doctrine.

Paul the Apostle of the Gentiles

Paul is a Jew but writes for the Gentiles mostly (Romans 11:13). He did minister to the Jews simultaneously, which explains why he could also do signs and wonders by the Spirit of God. However, there is a mixing of both Jewish and Christian doctrines because the apostles were trained by Jesus for the Jewish community initially. Jesus' ministry comprised of both the end-time physical Jew and the spiritual Christian.

Paul wrote the majority of scriptures that apply to the spiritual Christian Church.

Whether writings from Jesus or the apostles should contradict Paul, then it applies to a different group of people at a different time frame. This is how you read the Bible!

Matthew to John applies to the Jews. (Although Jesus introduces spiritual doctrines and salvation by faith alone and the spiritual kingdom of God).

Also, in Acts and the General Epistles from James to Revelation, this applies to the Jews. If anything in these books contradicts Paul, it is an end-time Jewish doctrine.

A Mystery Kept Secret

Paul's Gospel is new; its part of Jesus' preaching, which was kept a secret since the world began (Romans 16:25). Also, Paul writes about a mystery in Romans 11:25.

According to Paul, salvation is by faith without works, and a person is still saved no matter what sin is committed.

Unlike the Jews, in the Old Testament, they were afraid of losing their salvation when they sinned. Paul says you are saved by faith irrespective of whether you see yourself saved after evil deeds. In Romans 11:6, Paul makes a clear distinction between works and grace salvation.

"And grieve not the holy spirit of God, whereby ye are sealed unto the day of redemption". (Ephesians 4:30).

The Rapture

- Jesus taught a rapture occurs after the tribulation for the Jews (*post-tribulation, for the tribulation saints*).

- Paul taught of a rapture before the tribulation (*pre-tribulation Rapture*) for the Christians at the end of the Church age. (1 Thess 5:9 and Corinthians 15:51-52).

Paul's Good News Gospel and the Christians

John the Baptist ministry was predominantly Jewish. (Acts 19:1-3).

God is done with the Jews, but He will still save Israel in the future. It is temporary that they have been made blind to the truth so that the gentiles can be factored into God's family too. (Romans 11:26) "*until the fullness of the Gentiles become in*".

God will never break his promise to Abraham, and he will use physical Israel again very soon.

We, as Christians, do not go by the law for our salvation. And we do not follow Jewish physical diets, rules of the Mosaic Law, days of observances are no longer applicable.

The Old Testament prophesied that the Messiah comes as Sufferer and as King. Hence, the first and second coming of Christ.

The foundation of our Christian doctrines is in Romans to Philemon.

The Second Coming - Tribulation

The post-tribulation Rapture is for Tribulation saints, not Christians, because the Church is Rapture before the tribulation, at the end of the church age.

Millennium Kingdom

The prophecy of the Messiah as King comes to pass, at last. And works for salvation, *not faith*, is in this time frame.

I hope you see that proper division of the Bible is necessary to read and understand it.

It is bit like saying in old England people were punished by death for stealing but in modern times, punishment is minor, perhaps by imprisonment.

There is no contradiction is there?

Both are true in accordance with the time frame, right?

How To Get Saved?

———

We all must be born again, and this is how you can be saved. We have heard it so many times from so many leaders!

The Lord is my shepherd; I shall not want. He makes me lie down in green pastures. He leads me beside still waters. He restores my soul; He guides me in paths of righteousness for his name's sake.

He satisfies me with his presence, and my bones thrive like a well-watered garden. He leads me beside still waters.

He restores my soul. (Psalms 23:1–3)

How can you be saved?

Some people ask this question, and it is like a piece of cake to be saved.

It is a matter of asking Jesus to forgive you for your sins, past, present, and future sins, to believe from the heart, and all their sins are gone. It is not just saying a prayer, but once you are saved, you are always saved, forever and ever.

After you ask Jesus into your life, build a relationship with Jesus, and study the Bible, the Holy Spirit will take of the rest. You will still not be perfect on earth, but gradually, the Holy Spirit changes you.

I am here to tell you how to get saved in the easiest way possible. However, many people have frowned upon this method because they do not understand it fully.

You do not need to be perfect to get saved. Some people say you must first begin reading the Bible. You must do this and that. If you haven't read the Bible yet, get a Bible, turn to it every day and pray each day to show your love for God. When you pray, ask God that he shower his love on you and your loved ones.

If you are not a reader, fine, don't be discouraged. Because one day, when you are about to die *[maybe even if the world is about to end]*, there will be a review of everything that has passed here on earth. God knows your heart and your intentions.

If you are so talented or intelligent, why don't you read the Bible on your own? If you can't read it, why not ask someone else to read it for you so that you can follow along?

It's the best thing to do with your time and energy because when you have a daily bible reading, you will suddenly know something better if it is hard for some people to believe that they can start reading anytime and get saved.

I am not asking you to read the Bible for a year, a day, or even a few days. I am suggesting that you will find it helpful to start reading small chapters or verses of the Bible every day or each week and pray each day.

Because one day when you have completed your task in reading it, suddenly you will be able to understand the times of trouble that is going on around this world. You will get closer to God by reading parts, if not all, of the Bible.

But if you don't like reading, try listening to audiobooks and videos on YouTube. You have access to it, and it's free. It is so interesting, and there is so much to learn. I will recommend a few channels that I learned from later on in the back of this book.

But for now, you will be able to see clearly in your minds what is happening in our society here on earth right now. Through the Bible, you will know how can Christ minister to people who are having problems, such as what Satan did in modern society.

One day, you can know things better than I could ever tell you right now.

More people should be telling God how much they love him and how much they appreciate him for taking care of them.

Our parents, who have lived a long life and have found God after many years of searching, should be telling their kids how wonderful God is and how much he loves us. Perhaps you will to your children, even if they have grown up? Pass this book onto them to read or buy a copy for someone special in your life, a dear friend perhaps, who needs to be saved now.

Robert Breaker YouTube video (must watch!)

How To Get Saved:

https://bit.ly/34bDBr8

See also YouTube video Robert Breaker Salvation:

https://bit.ly/2RIv7VL

Who Is Jesus Christ According To The Bible?

———

J esus Christ is the Son of God or God in the flesh. He is all-loving and kind, patient and merciful, full of forgiveness.

God is all-powerful and a master magician, Creator of all things. God reveals himself through Jesus Christ to his children. Jesus was born of a virgin Mary; he grew up becoming a carpenter like his father Joseph, a carpenter.

Jesus was a Jew from Nazareth, and he was the Son of Mary, a young girl who lived in Galilee, an area that was part of the Roman province of Syria. Mary's parents were not poor, but they suffered significant want from poverty. Jesus as a child grew up with his family in Nazareth, where they struggled to make ends meet.

At Jesus' baptism, he spoke about his mission and how he would suffer for his people. At age 30, he performed many miracles at Jewish festivals, like when "lepers were cured" and "the deaf heard." The Romans also executed Jesus.

He died a cruel death on the cross, a punishment for his blasphemy at age 30. His body was taken by Joseph Arimathea (Matthew 27:57 & Mark 15:43); to be buried in a tomb. Contrary to the laws of Judaism law, Jesus was laid in a grave without any funeral rites.

Jesus did not claim to be God or God' Son; He was God's chosen and anointed messenger sent to show people how to live and love each other. Jesus' goal was to bring all people together as one loving family.

He taught according to his Father's teaching preserved in the writings of Moses and other prophets. Jesus never claimed divinity or deity, but he said: "All power has been given me in heaven and on earth. "*Go ye therefore and teach all nations, baptising them in the name of the Father, and the Son, and the Holy Ghost.*" Matthew 28:19

Jesus had a plan for eternal life as King, but he was crucified before implementing his plan. Jesus said to Nicodemus: "*Ye must be born again. Ye have heard that they said it of old time, thou shalt not kill; whosoever shall kill shall be in danger of the judgment. I say unto thee thou shalt not die but the way.*"

Jesus died on the cross as an innocent victim; he was to die in place of the sin of all people. Jesus' death was painful and tragic. He died for these sins, and by his sacrificial blood, Jesus was resurrected at age 33, just how God wanted him to be brought back from the dead.

Jesus came to give people life after they have died. Resurrection means that Jesus is alive forevermore and that he's ascended into his Heavenly Father's presence.t be changed."

Having become human flesh by virtue of his virgin birth, having suffered as a man on Earth, Jesus Christ made atonement for sin through his death on Calvary's Cross at age 33.

Jesus Is Everywhere In The Bible

———

Why is it that the Bible has many different names?

Why is a childlike Jesus called Yahushua?

What does the Bible say about Jesus?

What kind of person is Jesus?

Jesus, the Son of God: From God's Word, we can see that Yeshua was God, without beginning and an end. Thus, we can safely say that Jesus was not only the Son of God; He was also God Himself.

When Jesus spoke, He had to speak the words that God gave Him. If Jesus spoke of Himself as an angel, this makes no sense. Why would an angel talk down to us? Because God told him to do as such. God did not expect that His Son should be treated as a common person. An average human being should have been treated like a normal human being, just another ordinary person on earth.

God's plan for mankind was perfect and perfect people were expected in the Kingdom of Heaven. But if Mary, the mother of Yeshua, had conceived a child in the usual way through sexual intercourse between a man and a woman, then Yeshua would be an ordinary human being.

A person with two human parents (Yahweh-Father and Mary-Mother) cannot be God. If He was just an ordinary human being, He could not have taken away our sins on the cross. His death on the cross was only made possible because He was God Himself, sent to die for you and me.

If Yeshua were just an ordinary person, God would not have done what He did on the cross. If He had been just an ordinary man, He would not have taken away our sin by dying His death. The Cross of Jesus shows that God is a loving God, a God that is merciful and kind to mankind.

No one in the Bible except Jesus died for us, as did Jesus on the Cross.

Finding God

———

A common question that I have been asked in recent months is, "*How do we find God?*"

As we are all aware, the Bible is the book [and one volume] that God gave to us for our instruction. It says in Proverbs 3:13-15 that, "Thy Word is a lamp unto my feet and a light unto my path. Through thy Word, I have understood how great things thou hast done; and will do again."

The Bible will not lead you astray. It is a guide that teaches us about God, our relationship with him, and how to achieve our calling in life. For example, it teaches us that we should be Christians at heart to inherit eternal life. However, it also says that some seek a sign and will not believe because God has not given them the indication.

One of the most incredible things about reading your Bible is that God will speak directly to you, not as if he were a voice in your head, but as if he were right next to you. I used to joke with people that God would become very quiet once they had stopped going to Church and reading the Bible.

As I was reading the Bible, God spoke to me one day and said, "the reason people do not believe is that they do not read my book."

He then explained that parts of the Bible tend to get skipped over or overlooked when reading it. It is these parts that God tries to draw our attention towards.

For instance, when it says in Matthew 20:1-16 that Jesus had made a vineyard and hired labourers to work in it for the whole day for a denarius [a full day's wage].

The workers complained about not getting their fair share, and they said, "if you paid us more, we would work harder. Give us more money."

———————————

AS A RESULT OF THIS, the owner decided to hire more workers and increased their wages. However, there was no increase in the amount of work that the workers did. As a result, the owner fired all the workers and put people to work who would do their job. This is why it is essential to be paid for what you do rather than for how much you do it.

God also pointed out that when we read 1 Samuel, chapter 28, verse 8 that it states, "for thou art, not a God that hath pleasure in wickedness: neither shall evil dwell with thee.

The Lord will not give thy [Isaac's] enemies [that is, the Philistines] into thine hand; for thou art not a God of tumult nor a man of war."

The devil is the master of all disturbance. He wants everyone and everything to be in turmoil, fighting, unhappy and unfulfilled. He will do everything in his power to keep people from doing what God has called them to do.

For instance, he will start a war or start an argument between two people who can't get along with each other just so that they can't have peace and harmony in their lives. He will also try to keep you from doing what God has called you to do.

To accomplish this, the devil comes in all shapes and sizes.

Some of his most common features are:

1.A spirit of fear. This means that he will try to deceive you into believing that there is something that God is unwilling or unable to do for you if you receive it from him. Still, in reality, there is no such thing as a spirit of fear, for Jesus says that "I am the Lord thy God which teaches thee" (Isaiah 54:13).

2.A spirit of bondage. This means that he will try to convince you that something is holding you back from becoming the person God has called you to be in life. Still, in reality, this desire for things to be different from what they are is nothing more than a selfish desire because Satan is an enemy of God and wants you to fight against him.

3.A spirit of fear again - this time fear about the future. He will also try to convince you that nothing can be done about your present condition. Still, I tell you today that God has always been concerned about us and our situation.

4.A spirit of pride means that he wants us to think we are good enough on our own and help us believe so by trying to convince us that we don't need anything from God.

However, the truth of the matter is we can do nothing without God. Isaiah 64:6 says, "O Lord, thou art our father; we are the clay, and thou our potter; and we all are the work of thy hand."

5.A spirit of witchcraft. This is where the devil will tell you that you can't do anything with what you have to offer for God. Still, in reality, we can do anything with what we have if we believe in God's ability to use it for his purpose. In John 6:44, it says, "No man can come to me except the Father which hath sent me draw him..."

6.A spirit of unbelief - this means that he will try to convince you that you don't have the ability or endurance to see your prayers answered. But in reality, if anyone can overcome such a spirit, it believes in Jesus Christ. In Matthew 17:20, it says, "If ye have faith as a grain of mustard seed, ye shall say unto this mountain, Remove hence to yonder place, and it shall remove."

The devil also operates in the same manner in the Church. He will try to stir up disagreements between Christians to fight against each other instead of fighting against the devil. Among other things, he is responsible for keeping Christians from doing what God has called them to do.

Therefore, if you are a Christian and don't feel like your life reflects your calling, you will probably be held back by the devil because you don't believe in yourself. Be encouraged to believe in Jesus Christ and the power he has given us over the devil. Don't let Satan give you a spirit of helplessness that will prevent you from doing what you know God has called you to do.

Although the devil is very active in this world, he doesn't have as much power as some might think. His primary purpose is to lead people away from God. Still, he was created by God for that purpose and therefore is limited by God's laws of creation.

However, there are a few things that he doesn't have to do because he was created to do.

These things are listed below:

1. He can't create a new soul or a new spirit in that person. (see Genesis 1:31 for more information).

2. He can't change another person's mind about God or what they should do with their lives. We human beings can do this and therefore can choose whether to follow God's Will in our own lives or not.

3. He can't make a person stop believing in God or stop believing in Jesus Christ.

4. He can't make a person turn away from the truth that Jesus Christ offers them. Some people just don't want to hear the truth and will do everything they can to fight against it, but that doesn't change the fact that Jesus Christ is their only way to heaven.

5. He can't keep a person from hearing or reading about the Gospel of Jesus Christ even if it means they have to go out of their way so others won't bother them with it.

6. He can't make Christians go back on their commitment to Jesus Christ.

7. He can't make a person stop loving others. Jesus said, "If you love those who love you, what credit is that to you? Even sinners love those who love them." (Luke 6:32)

8. He can't make His followers give up on following Him by being beaten or threatened with death or even by being killed for their faith in Him.

(John 16:32 NKJV)

9. He can't be stopped by anything; nothing can separate us from Jesus.

(Romans 8:35-39 - NKJV)

10. Jesus' work in this world cannot be stopped or stopped by anyone!

(I Peter 4:12 - NKJV)

The Holy Trinity Explained

———

The Holy Trinity is the central mystery of Christian faith and worship. It refers to God's act of self-giving love for us, in which he lavishes us with his life-giving presence.

The Father sends Jesus, his eternal Son and Word made flesh; he sends the Holy Spirit.

All three are intimately one in giving their lives for our salvation. In this way, God has reconciled all things to himself in Christ (2 Corinthians 5:18–20).

The Holy Trinity is God

the Father, the Son and the womanly Spirit (Holy Spirit) (who helps us understand). There's no female god.

It is tough to explain because nobody knows what it means. It's pretty simple, though; God is in three persons, but each person has only one nature. The Holy Trinity has no beginning and no end, and the persons are all equal. Something like that.

I hope that that was helpful for you. If not, I'm sorry, but this is all I can tell you. Love and peace to you!

The Holy Trinity is God manifested in three forms: Father, Son (Jesus) and the Holy Spirit). The Father rules over the universe with wisdom and strength. The Son is born of a virgin and rules over all creation with great wisdom, strength and love; The Holy Spirit guides all creation into Christ.

They are not three separate gods but different ways of God. The Father is the first person of the Trinity because he created us and knows us best through his Son Jesus. The Son died for us and rose again for our salvation. We worship him as a god by doing what he has told us to do on earth: love one another, help the poor and so on. That's why we call him 'God', but he is not one God but three gods, the Father, Son and Holy Spirit.

There is no other God but the Father, Son and Holy Spirit. God is a trinity: the Father created the world, Jesus Christ came to earth as a man and suffered for all our sins, and the Holy Spirit guides us.

Both Jesus Christ and God (the Father) are uncreated because they always existed. The Scriptures say that God is Spirit (John 4:24) and that He, therefore, must not be a man.

He has no beginning and no end. Jesus Christ is God incarnate, as the Apostle John records, "In the beginning was the Word, and the Word was with God, and the Word was God. And the Word became flesh and dwelt among us, full of grace..." (John 1:1-2). The Holy Spirit is a Person who also proceeds from God.

The Holy Trinity are one in three but three in one; each has a different task to perform for the sake of humanity. After all, Jesus did come to earth and die on the cross so that we could live, and it was the Holy Spirit who gave Jesus the strength to do this. So, Christ's death was not in vain, but his death was for us.

The Holy Trinity is God in three persons: Father, Son, and Holy Spirit, with each having a different duty: The Father is chief over humankind while Jesus is charged with redeeming man.

The Holy Spirit is our comforter and teacher. Each person has one nature: God's divine nature for the Father and Son; human nature for Jesus Christ; and divine-human nature for the Holy Spirit.

The Holy Trinity is God in 3 persons/elements:

The Father, the Son and the Holy Spirit. They are all one God in three Persons. Each has one divine nature but exists with a distinct Person. The Father is eternal, omnipotent, and omniscient. The Son is eternal, incarnate of the Virgin Mary while He was sinless; the Holy Spirit proceeds from both immediately after Jesus' ascension into heaven. He sent the Holy Spirit to His disciples. Thus, each has a distinct role in performing God's plan for our salvation.

The Holy Trinity:

God created mankind but was not satisfied by it, so he wanted to visit his creation which he could do through Christ (because he is God). So, God, the father, chooses Jesus as his Son and the Holy Spirit as his helper. He told Jesus to go back to earth and show mankind what is right. And when he died on the cross, it was the Holy Spirit that helped him get up again to show mankind that death is not the end but only an entrance to a new life.

God, The Father:

Eternal, omnipotent Creator of all things; who sent His Son Jesus Christ into the world to be our saviour from spiritual death on the cross. He sent His Holy Spirit into our hearts (our minds) at baptism to teach us all things about God through prayer and worship.

Passages Of Paul In The New Testament

———

I Corinthians 15:1-5

Now I make known unto you, brethren, the Gospel which I preached unto you, which also ye have received, and wherein ye stand;

2 By which ye are saved if ye keep in memory what I preached unto you unless ye have believed in vain.

3 For I delivered unto you first of all that which I also received, how that Christ died for our sins according to the scriptures;

4 And that he was buried, and that he rose again the third day according to the scriptures;

5 And that he was seen of Cephas, then of the twelve: After that, he was seen of above five hundred brethren at once; of whom many remain unto this present, but some are fallen asleep.

I Corinthians 15:3

Now I make known unto you, brethren, the Gospel which I preached unto you, which also ye have received, and wherein ye stand;

I Corinthians 15:12

Now I make known unto you, brethren, the Gospel which I preached unto you, which also ye have received, and wherein ye stand; After that Jesus was seen of above five hundred brethren at once; of whom many remain unto this present day, but some are fallen asleep.

I Corinthians 15:1-8

I make known unto you, brethren, the Gospel which I preached unto you, which also ye have received and wherein ye stand;

2 By which ye are saved if ye keep in memory what I preached unto you unless ye have believed in vain. For I delivered unto you first of all that which I also received, how that Christ died for our sins according to the scriptures;

3 And that he was buried, and that he rose again the third day according to the scriptures;

4 And that he was seen of Cephas, then of the twelve:

5 After that, he was seen of above five hundred brethren at once; of whom many remain unto this present day, but some are fallen asleep.

Blood Atonement

———

The blood of Jesus Christ washes away the sins and blemishes of our persons and cleanses us of all unrighteousness. Therefore, throughout the New Testament, we see that people should seek to be reconciled to God through repentance (2 Corinthians 5:17; Acts 3:19-20; Ephesians 2:8-9; 1 John 1:9).

The expression "atonement" is a technical term for what the Reformers called the sacrifice of Christ. The Word is used three times in the New Testament:

(1) to describe Christ's anticipated sacrifice (Matthew 20:28; Mark 10:45), (2) to describe Christ's accomplished sacrifice ("The blood of Christ, who through the eternal Spirit offered himself without blemish to God, will cleanse your conscience from dead works to serve the living God" - Hebrews 9:14), and

(3) by Peter about his sin of denying Jesus three times on the night of his arrest and crucifixion (1 Peter 1:18-19).

Passages such as Hebrews 9:22 indeed describe Jesus' death as a means by which God provided purification for sins committed after baptism.

This is known as "satisfaction," not atonement. Satisfaction was employed to spare Israel from the wrath of God in the Old Testament. But it was not a payment for sins to satisfy God's justice and wrath. The people were given animal sacrifices to express remorse and reconnect with God. The work of Christ was a fulfilment of that particular type of sacrifice.

Where does this leave us in a theological context, when the book of Hebrews, often hailed as the best-attested book in the New Testament. It invokes passages such as 1 John 1:7 and 2 Corinthians 5:21 to suggest that Christ's atonement was not for personal sin. In this regard, we must look to other New Testament writings that indicate otherwise.

For example, the book of Revelation records that Jesus died as a sacrifice for sin "to show his righteousness" (3:1) and "for the sins of those who are to believe in me" (2:23). It seems that despite all that the Protestant Reformers did to encourage individual repentance and forgiveness, on at least one issue, they were wrong.

As Eugene Peterson notes in The Message Bible, "There's no getting around it: **blood was involved**." And that's particularly true if you're looking for divine forgiveness.

There's no other way into God's presence except through the blood of his Son.

See also YouTube video Robert Breaker Salvation:

https://bit.ly/2RIv7VL

How Do We Pray To God?

———

C hristians pray to God, who is the most high and powerful. To pray means to worship God by using words, like speaking.

Prayer

Prayer is a way of communicating with God. Prayer allows Christians to speak with God in a way that we feel comfortable because they come from their hearts and directly communicate with God. According to the Bible, we should speak comfortably with God through prayer and share our needs and prayers with other people.[1]

How do we pray?

The method of praying has changed over the years as well as it does now. The Bible does not give us many details on praying, so we need to learn and study other people's experiences. How do you believe that you should pray? Here are some Bible quotes about prayer:

John 15:7-8 (NIV) - "If you abide in me, and my words abide in you, ask whatever you wish, and it will be done for you. By this, My Father is glorified, who has chosen you [Christians] that you may be ['his'] own [owned]."

Romans 10:10 (NIV) - "For with the heart one believes [and prays] unto God, and with the mouth [i.e., in prayer] we confess [or hold accountable] our sins."

Romans 12:1-2 (NIV) - "I appeal to you, therefore, brothers and sisters, by the mercies of God, to present your bodies ['ready for death'] a living sacrifice ['willing]"].

Colossians 4:2 (NIV) - "And pray in the Spirit on all occasions with all kinds of prayers and requests.

Romans 8:26 - "Likewise the Spirit also helps in our weaknesses. For we do not know what we should pray for as we ought, but the Spirit Himself makes intercession for us with groanings which cannot be uttered.

Philippians 4:6-7 (NIV) - "Be anxious for nothing, but in everything by prayer and supplication with thanksgiving let your requests be made known to God. And the peace of God, which surpasses all understanding, will guard your hearts and your minds in Christ Jesus."

2 Thessalonians 3:1 (NIV) - "Finally, brethren, pray for us that the word of the Lord may have free course and be glorified, even as it is with you."

1 Corinthians 14:15 (NIV) - "What is it then? I will pray with the Spirit, and I will also pray with the mind.

1 Thessalonians 5:17 (KJV) - "Pray without ceasing."

Jeremiah 29:12 (NIV) - "I know the plans I have for you,' declares the LORD, 'plans to prosper you and not to harm you, plans to give you hope and a future."

Matthew 21:22-23 (NIV) - "And whatever you ask in prayer, you will receive, if you have faith.

Hell Is Real

————

S in is real. There is no doubt that the Bible says some rather severe things about sin, and we are told in Scripture that our sin will bring us to hell.

What? What kind of a place is hell?

Can we go there?

If so, what would it feel like?

Is hell a literal place?

Or is it merely an idea, a concept that some have held over the centuries?

Hell is not just an idea or something; you can be burned into a few pages of text.

Hellish consequences are genuine both on this earth and in the eternal future. We can do many things, or fail to do, which will make hell real in our lives. Unfortunately, there are many things that we could have done but did not do, and for those things, we will be judged.

How about you?

Do you know if hell is real?

And if so, what does it look like?

Can you describe it?

How would you feel being in a place like that?

Would you even want to think about it much beyond this very moment?

Or would you want the mere thought of it to disappear entirely out of your mind constantly?

If hell is real, the devil is real, and he has a plan for us to get us to hell to torture us in the lake of fire.

The devil has told a lot of people a lot of things, which may not be true. The devil wants to deceive people and take as many souls with him to hell as possible when he is cast into the lake of fire.

It would be wise for you to examine what it is that he would have you believe. And most importantly, what it is precisely that he does NOT want you to know about Jesus Christ's sacrifice for your sin.

So many people today claim that hell is not real at all that it's just a myth created by religious fanatics to keep their members in line through an irrational fear of a place they've never even seen.

The devil understands that some people will not believe hell is real unless they are first frightened out of their minds and convinced that hell would be a horrible place. The devil wants to have his way in getting us to his evil purposes. And fear is the best way to accomplish that.

It is a very real and very frightening truth that w God's eternal fire can damn us. We can also be saved from this torment by accepting Jesus Christ as our saviour and trusting him with our lives forever. There is no greater love than a man who would lay down his very life for another person's sins, especially if his sacrifice is something the person can never repay ever.

And that is what Jesus Christ did for us. He willingly laid down his life for us, and we had better take advantage of that! The sinful man in the Garden of Eden could have refused God's offer to be obedient and become a righteous human being.

Still, he couldn't have known that he would be damned to eternal torment on the day of judgment if he had accepted God's offer. And if Jesus Christ had not offered to die for our sins, then we would have had no hope of being saved from this torment any time in the future, and no one would have ever heard of him or his love for us.

You see, whether you live forever or suffer eternity in hell, it's your call. You must choose to do what Jesus would want you to do. If you don't know him, he would want you to believe in him as your saviour and then follow him with all of your heart until you die.

God will not send anyone to hell because he wants them there. He wants us all in heaven. God's intentions have always been for us to share eternity with Him in Heaven and not in eternal torment. God loves each one of his children, and he sent his Son Jesus Christ into the world so that we could be forgiven for our sins and live forever in paradise with him in heaven in his presence in the eternal light of God's presence.

If you are not saved today, then it is time to decide to follow Jesus Christ. Jesus is waiting for you. His arms are open wide to receive you as a special treasure, one whom he loves and cares for above all others, his own Son!

Take a moment now and ask him to forgive you of your sins today and allow his grace and mercy to cover you forevermore. It may be the most crucial decision any man ever makes in life if he lives or dies.

Our Lord Jesus Christ died on the cross, taking away our sins forever and forevermore. He was buried and rose from the dead three days later to give us eternal life with him, a life with no more pain, sorrow, or death. And he still loves us today.

He's waiting for you right now to accept his love and eternal grace that he freely offers us all! You can call on him to come into your heart and change your life forever!

All you have to do

All you have to do is ask him to forgive you of your sins and make you a child of God. May God grant you a heart full of love for his Son Jesus Christ and the wisdom to accept his grace and mercy by asking Jesus Christ to be your saviour right now.

And know that Jesus loves you forevermore. Amen!

Father in heaven, this person came to read your Son's book and has a desire to learn more about Jesus Christ. We pray that you would open his heart to your Son's grace and forgiveness today and save him from eternal torment in hell.

We thank you for the gift of salvation you offer all men, even me but especially this man, whom we don't even know by name. Help him find salvation with Jesus Christ today, where it is found only through faith in Your Son, Lord Jesus Christ himself! In the name of Jesus, we pray.

Amen.

How to be saved:

To be saved, simply confess with your mouth the Lord Jesus Christ as your saviour, and believe in your heart that God raised him from the dead. Then God will give you eternal life.

You can pray this prayer to ask Jesus to save you right now:

"Dear Lord Jesus, I am a sinner. I believe you died for my sins and rose again on the third day. I open the door of my life and receive you as my Saviour and Lord. Thank You for forgiving me of all

my sins and giving me eternal life. Come into my heart right now. Make me the kind of person you want me to be.

In Jesus' name, Amen."

"Dear Lord Jesus, I know you are coming soon. I need to be prepared for your return. Please forgive me of all my sins, and come into my heart. Make me the kind of person you want me to be. In Jesus' name, Amen."

"Dear Lord Jesus, thank you for dying for me on the cross. I accept your gift of salvation and love. I am ready to go home to be with my saviour in heaven and with my family and friends in heaven. Thank you for forgiving me of all my sins and giving me eternal life. In Jesus' name, Amen."

"Dear Lord Jesus, thank you for coming back to earth as a man so that you can save all people from their sins. I want to be saved because I need your forgiveness and love in my life. Thank you for taking me like your Son, but more than that, as the Son of God. In Jesus' name, Amen.

"Dear Father in Heaven, I am lost. I have sinned and am breaking all your laws. Please, teach me your way. Help me to repent and give me a love for my fellow man. Save me as only you, the true God can do. In Jesus' name, Amen."

"God, thank you for sending your Son Jesus to die on the cross for my sins. Thank you for forgiving me of all that is past and present because of Jesus' death on the cross. Thank you, Lord God Almighty! In Jesus' name, I pray this Amen.

What Is Heaven Like?

———

A lot of Christians seem to think that a heaven is a place on earth. That's not the case. Heaven is a distinct location in a distant dimension of the universe. Compared to heaven, the earth as we know it is nothing more than a drop in the ocean or like an ant compared to an elephant.

And God does not want us to think that he is only on earth. He has other plans for us, expectantly waiting for us in heaven. So, we need to get used to the idea that heaven is not here on earth but somewhere out there in space and time.

Where is Heaven?

Heaven is located where God wants it to be. It could be in a dimension so far away that one may never know where it is.

If God were to place heaven in the space of this universe, humankind would surely "finder" and build rockets to go there. So there lies the problem, it's hidden from us so we can't discover it.

This is because God doesn't want us running around doing whatever we want when we get to heaven. Heaven is like an exclusive club; you must prove yourself worthy of being a member first before giving access.

The Pre-Tribulation Rapture Of The Church

———

The pre-tribulation Rapture of the Church is an eschatological doctrine that the (first) resurrection will occur before the tribulation. It contrasts to 'post-tribulation rapture', which occurs after the tribulation, but before the second resurrection.

The pre-tribulation Rapture of the Church concludes that only believers will be resurrected at this point, leaving all other people un-resurrected until after the tribulation has ended.

This would include unborn babies and other individuals who were not Christian during Christ's ministry. Adventists maintain that re-births are unnecessary for such individuals. They gain entire spiritual life during the 1000 years of human history that will survive the tribulation.

The pre-tribulation Rapture of the Church refers to a future event where the Christian holy ones will be raptured (carried up) into heaven at some point before the Great Tribulation. This event is commonly held to occur just before the Great Tribulation. However, some believe that it is a future event after the Church has been persecuted and martyred for a few years.

Christians will be taken up into heaven before the second coming of Jesus Christ for some time. This is referred to as the

"Rapture" (borrowing from Rev. 4:1). When Jesus does come back and takes His Bride away (takes them to Heaven with Him), it is referred to as the "catching away" or the "taking up. " This is not a general physical resurrection, but rather the metaphorical removal of the Christians to Heaven.

At the time of the Rapture, we would be told that we will see "the Son of Man coming in a cloud" (Matt 24:30), and then "Suddenly, he's there", and let's "Come with him". Because of this, some Adventists hold that the Rapture will occur at any moment, while others teach that it is a future event.

Though there are differing views on what will happen between the first resurrection and the second resurrection or tribulation, this is one view mentioned many times in the New Testament. I will provide links to specific and further explanations and full proof about this later in the back of this book to further research for yourself.

Watch Robert Breaker YouTube video The Rapture of the Church:

https://tinyurl.com/TheRaptureoftheChurch

Listen Free Audio below:

Dr Andy Woods explains The Rapture of the Church: https://bit.ly/3vq1Fmc

50 Fun Facts About The Bible

———

- The Bible is also known as the Gospel, the Old Testament, or simply the Bible. It contains 30 books written from different perspectives and at other times. Scriptures believed to be inspired by God appear in red. The oldest part of the Bible is the books of Moses, written around 1200 BC.

- Some notable authors include Job, Daniel, Ezra, and Matthew (also known as "the tax collector"), all canonised between 400-400 BC. The New Testament canonising recognised Jesus as the Son of God.

- The Bible is much more than just a collection of books. The Bible comprises 66 separate books, 31 in the Old Testament and 35 in the New Testament. However, it is not simply a collection of books, but it is considered one book with different sections, called "books."

- The Bible contains amazing stories, like when Joshua ordered the sun and the moon to stop moving. Jonah went into the belly of a whale for three days, similar to when Jesus died for three days was buried and rose again. Abraham lied about having a wife named Sarah. (Genesis 25:1-5).

- The Bible contains many prophecies that have already been fulfilled and that will be fulfilled. The Bible contains many prophecies that have yet to be fulfilled. It is written in the Bible: "I saw all that he had done, and how merciful he was...but I have more witnesses than all of them for the Lord has inspired all his prophets from Samuel and his servants to this day" (Acts 7:12-13).

- There are many different sects in the Bible - There are many other sects of Bible believers. According to Paul, there will be many different groups dividing the Christians. "Do I now persuade men or God? Or do I seek to please men?" (Romans 9:20).

- The Bible is considered holy - Most people consider the Bible to be holy, and it is, of course. There is a superstition that if you write your name with its first letter in the Bible, it will bring good luck.

- The Bible is an ancient book written and edited or compiled by many men over a long period.

- Ingenious Sumerian and Babylonian scribes invented the serial numbering of chapters and verses so that the scrolls could be read in order. This invention was copied by Jewish scribes when they translated the scrolls into Hebrew around 400 BC.

- The Bible is an international bestseller. It has been translated into more than 1,100 languages and dialects.

- The oldest surviving Hebrew manuscript of the complete Old Testament is about 1,000 years older than the oldest previously known manuscript. This discovery was made in the Dead Sea Scrolls.

- The Bible was written by 40 different authors living in other areas and times over 1500 years.
- The Bible contains 32 books written by 15 authors over 1,500 years.

- The last book of the Bible was written around 95 A.D. The first book of the Old Testament was written around 1450 BC. (This does not include the apocryphal books.)

- Every one of the sixty-six books in our English New Testament has been preserved. Still, there are thousands and thousands of alternate readings in the various ancient manuscripts. The task has been left to scholars to decide which readings are authentic.

- The Bible was originally written in Hebrew, Aramaic and Greek. The earliest manuscripts of each Testament are in Hebrew. The oldest Greek manuscripts were from the third century A.D.; the earliest translations were into Latin and Syriac in the second century A.D.

- The book of Ruth was initially written in Hebrew,

but it has been preserved only in our English Bible.

- The books of the Bible are arranged according to their content. The first six books have been given the names of the letters in the Hebrew alphabet.

- A two-letter chapter is known as a parashah. A four-letter chapter is known as a mezuzah. Each book of the Bible has been divided up into 31 two-letter and 49 four-letter chapters.

- The prophets Haggai, Zechariah and Malachi are the final three books of the Old Testament.

- Because it was written in Greek, the book of Revelation is not part of the Jewish canon. Still, it is considered inspired by many Christians and accepted as canonical Scripture by all four Gospels (Revelation 1:1).

- The twenty-fourth chapter of Matthew's Gospel records Jesus' genealogy. It has been preserved only in our English Bible.
- The book of Hebrews is a letter from Paul to the Church in Rome. It has been preserved only in our English Bible.

- The first seven chapters of Romans have been preserved only in our English Bible.

- The Bible contains both history and fiction, moral

lessons and poetry. The Bible is the most influential book in Western history. It has influenced cultures all over the world, including American culture.

- The Bible contains 27 versions of the Ten Commandments.

- The earliest English translation of the Bible was made in 1382 when John Wycliffe translated the New Testament. John Wycliffe was a religious reformer.
- Shakespeare and other early English writers used the Geneva Bible. It is the Bible most cited by modern-day authors.

- The King James Version of the Bible is the only translation of the Old Testament into English to retain all of the "thee and thou" forms of speech. It is one of the best Bibles to study.

- The Bible contains several conflicting and questionable accounts.

- All of the New Testament books are anonymous, written by authors without known credentials or backgrounds. The authors identify themselves as "inspired." This is supposed to make them more reliable and trustworthy.

- Origen (AD 185) was the most significant Biblical scholar in the early Church. He was a prolific author and translator of Greek works into Latin.

- Jerome (AD 347) is credited as the first to translate most of the New Testament into Latin (sometime between 383 and 405). He is considered the "father of the Catholic church."

- Martin Luther (AD 1509-1546) was a German priest and professor who began the Protestant Reformation being angry that the Catholic Church did not address issues like Pope Leo X's sale of indulgences.

- John Calvin (AD 1509-1564) was a French priest and professor who advocated a rigid interpretation of the Bible. He developed the theological system of Calvinism.

- John Wesley (AD 1703-1791) was a devout Anglican clergyman who founded Methodism. He based his theology on the Bible and the Bible alone.

- Sun Myung Moon (A.D. 1920-) is the founder of the Unification Church. He has written an interpretation of the Bible called the "Divine Principle."

- The King James Version is no longer in print. It was the first English-language translation of the Bible to appear. In 1611, it was published in England.

- The Douay-Rheims Version of the Bible was published in 1609 and also in 1752. The "Douay" refers to the English College at Douay, France.

- The Revised Standard Version was published in 1952. Subsequent texts were published in 1971 and 1984.
- The New American Bible was published in 1971. It is the first translation of the Roman Catholic Bible to be completed by Catholics in America.

- The New Jerusalem Bible was published in 1966. It is the first translation of the Roman Catholic Bible to be completed by Catholics in the United States.

- The New Revised Standard Version published in 1989. It is a revision of the Revised Standard Version (1952).
- The New International Version published in 1978. It is a revision of the International Bible Version (1958).

- The Holman Christian Standard Bible was published in 1997. It is an update of the Common English Bible (1995).

- Over the past two centuries, there have been many new English versions of the Bible. Modern technology has allowed multiple translation teams to work independently on their translations and then compare their works. This is how every reputable translation has taken place.

- The New American Standard Bible (NASB) is a two-volume translation of the Hebrew Scriptures from 1952 to 1963. There are currently over 140,000 copies in print. It is the most-used English version of the Bible outside the Church of England and Episcopal churches. It is the most widely used version of the Old Testament, second only to the King James Version.

- A fourteen-member translation team translated the New American Standard Bible under Walter J. Browning and Arthur L. Farstad. The first five translations were completed by the year 1952. The rest of the Old Testament was completed in a second round of translation work from 1951 to 1958. There are 70,000 copies in print. The New American Standard Bible was revised in 1963.

- The New Revised Standard Version is a new version of the Revised Standard Version (1952), based on the More English Bible of 1931. The New Revised Standard Version is a revision of the New American Standard Bible (1963).

- A twenty-member translation team translated the New Revised Standard Version under the direction of Robert Pierce and Gerald G. Hailey at The Lockman Foundation in Springfield, Missouri. The first five versions were completed in 1987 and 1988. The remaining Old Testament was completed in 1989; there are 60,000 copies in print.

BONUS FACT!

- The New Revised Standard Version was revised in 1993. Aside from some corrections in the original book of Samuel, the complete Bible translation stayed the same. The Old Testament Apocrypha was removed. Several other passages were changed to be more gender-inclusive.

Did You Know That

- *Psalm 118 is the middle chapter of the entire Bible?*
- *Psalm 117, before Psalm 118, is the shortest chapter in the Bible?*
- *Psalm 119, after Psalm 118, is the longest chapter in the Bible?*
- *The Bible has 594 chapters before Psalm 118 and 594 chapters after Psalm 118?*
- *If you add up all the chapters except Psalm 118, you get a total of 1188 chapters.*
- *1188 or Psalm 118, verse 8, is the middle verse of the entire Bible?*

Should the central verse not have an important message? "It is better to take refuge in the Lord than to trust in man." Psalm 118.8

Psalm 118 | Bible Teaching Notes. Ref: https://bibleteachingnotes.blog/2018/08/14/psalm-118/

ABC's Of Salvation

———

G ospel = Good News
Corinthians 15:1-4

ABC OF SALVATION

A - ADMIT

Admit you are a sinner and have made mistakes.

Romans 3:23

B - BELIEVE

Believe that Jesus is God's Son, died on the cross for you, and rose from the grave on the third day.

Romans 10:9-10

C - CONFESS

Confess with your mouth that Jesus is Lord of your life. Commit yourself to a life of following Jesus and serving others.

Romans 10:13

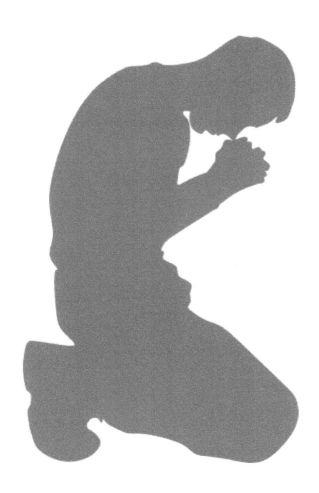

Useful Links

———

Top highly recommended teachers according to your style of learning:

1. Robert Breaker (Pastor/Missionary)

Website of Missionary Evangelist

https://thecloudchurch.org

Also, on YouTube

How To Get Saved: https://bit.ly/34bDBr8

Watch Robert Breaker

YouTube video (must watch!),

The Rapture of the Church:

https://tinyurl.com/TheRaptureoftheChurch

1. **Dr Andy Woods**

https://www.andywoodsministries.org/

Also, on YouTube

Listen Free Audio below:

Dr Andy Woods explains The Rapture of the Church: https://bit.ly/3vq1Fmc

1. **Pastor Gene Kim**

https://realbiblebelievers.com/about-us/pastor-gene-kim/

Also, on YouTube, Pastor Gene Kim explains dispensationalism: https://bit.ly/2RC3fTm

1. **JD Farag**

Bible Prophesy Updates, sermons and other resources:

https://www.jdfarag.org/

1. **Amir Tsarfati**

News from Israel and Bible Prophesy Updates.

https://beholdisrael.org/

https://www.youtube.com/user/beholdisrael/videos

Thank you again for your purchase.

I hope you found this book helpful and comforting. If so, please give us a thumbs-up; your review is most important to assist others in their Spiritual journey.

Thanking you in advance.

My Testimony

———

It was 15th October 2017, the year the Revelation 12 sign was revealed, many of us woke up (not Wokism!).

I was in the garden and the bright early afternoon sky turned very dark. It was almost like night; unlike anything I'd ever experienced. The atmosphere was heavy, and it was very eery. This got my curiosity, and I started searching for more information.

The media never seemed to report on this. Long story short, I began to learn more about the Revelation 12 Sign in the sky.

I soon began studying scriptures in the Bible and listening to hundreds of videos and pod casts. About a year before, I was extremely cross that I didn't read the Bible as much as I should have done and that it left me bewildered on where to begin and how to study it.

Over five years later, I can honestly say it now makes sense!

You see, I was born and raised a catholic, and I schooled in a prestigious private convent in Surrey, England. Educated in the Bible scriptures but only Matthew, Mark, Luke and John. That was it!

No one got to the book of Acts or the End Times in the book Revelation, which we often discussed in our break time. It seemed scary and confusing when reading about the beast rising out of the sea. We thought it would be a long way away, perhaps not in our lifetime even. But it isn't. It is almost here.

This is why I decided or rather felt compelled to write this book, to help save others. I always believed in God, in Jesus Christ, the Holy Trinity. I am a Bible-believing Christian, a born-again Evangelist now. I do not follow the catholic faith.

I always questioned why they had many statues, rituals; why did things the way they did, and now I know why. I could never understand the sermons because they were teaching a completely different doctrine meant for the Jews!

I am no longer with the Roman Catholic Church I am happy to say. I only follow what is in the Bible, predominantly the study guide version of the King James Bible. I finally learned about the Bible myself; praise Jesus for calling me, all glory to God.

I hope you find the information in this book of value, comfort, joy and hope. It is the only truth and promising joy in this world. Don't be deceived and be in darkness.

I wish you well on your journey to being saved because time is short and Jesus is coming soon – are you sealed, heaven-bound, and Rapture ready too?

This book has shown you how.

About The Author

—————

Anthea Peries BSc (Hons) is a published author; she completed her undergraduate studies in several sciences, including Biology, Brain and Behaviour and Child Development.

A former graduate member of the British Psychological Society, she has experience in counselling and is a former senior management executive.

Born in London, Anthea enjoys fine cuisine, writing and has travelled the world. She has a spoilt but cute but naughty black and white cat named Giorgio.

Other Books By This Author

———

You may be interested in other self-help books by Anthea Peries, particularly about bereavement, funerals, chemotherapy treatment, other areas such as eating disorders; food addiction, binge-eating, sugar cravings, emotional eating, or night eating syndrome, insomnia.

Don't miss out!

Visit the website below and you can sign up to receive emails whenever Anthea Peries publishes a new book. There's no charge and no obligation.

https://books2read.com/r/B-A-DMCG-FIDPB

BOOKS 2 READ

Connecting independent readers to independent writers.

Also by Anthea Peries

Cancer and Chemotherapy
Coping with Cancer & Chemotherapy Treatment: What You
Need to Know to Get Through Chemo Sessions
Coping with Cancer: How Can You Help Someone with
Cancer, Dealing with Cancer Family Member, Facing Cancer
Alone, Dealing with Terminal Cancer Diagnosis,
Chemotherapy Treatment & Recovery
Chemotherapy Survival Guide: Coping with Cancer &
Chemotherapy Treatment Side Effects
Chemotherapy Chemo Side Effects And The Holistic
Approach: Alternative, Complementary And Supplementary
Proven Treatments Guide For Cancer Patients
Chemotherapy Treatment: Comforting Gift Book For
Patients Coping With Cancer

Christian Books
Seeking Salvation, Secure In Belief: How To Get Sure-Fire
Saved By Grace Through Faith, Rapture Ready And Heaven
Bound
Thriving In Chaos: A Practical Guide To Surviving In A
World Of Uncertainty: Strategies and Tools for Building
Resilience, Finding Stability, and Flourishing in Turbulent
Times
Divine Mathematics: Unveiling the Secrets of Gematria
Exploring the Mystical & Symbolic Significance of
Numerology in Jewish and Christian Traditions, & Beyond

The Divine Library: A Short Comprehensive Summary Guide to the Bible: From Genesis to Revelation, Discover the Power, Purpose and Meaning of Scripture in the World's Most Influential Book

Daughters of Faith: The Untold Stories of Women of Power and Strength in the Bible| Rediscovering the Courage, Resilience, Belief And Trust of Females In Scripture

Paul The Apostle Of Christ: From Persecutor To Preacher Exploring the Life, Ministry, and Legacy of A Man Who Transformed Christianity, Spreading the Gospel Across the Mediterranean

Mastering Your Money: A Practical Guide to Budgeting and Saving For Christians Take Control of Your Finances and Achieve Your Financial Goals with 10 Simple Steps

Colon and Rectal

Bowel Cancer Screening: A Practical Guidebook For FIT (FOBT) Test, Colonoscopy & Endoscopic Resection Of Polyp Removal In The Colon

Cancer: Bowel Screening| A Simple Guide About How It Works To Help You Decide

Eating Disorders

Food Cravings: Simple Strategies to Help Deal with Craving for Sugar & Junk Food

Sugar Cravings: How to Stop Sugar Addiction & Lose Weight

The Immune System, Autoimmune Diseases & Inflammatory Conditions: Improve Immunity, Eating Disorders & Eating for Health

Food Addiction: Overcome Sugar Bingeing, Overeating on Junk Food & Night Eating Syndrome

Food Addiction: Overcoming your Addiction to Sugar, Junk Food, and Binge Eating

Food Addiction: Why You Eat to Fall Asleep and How to Overcome Night Eating Syndrome

Overcome Food Addiction: How to Overcome Food Addiction, Binge Eating and Food Cravings

Emotional Eating: Stop Emotional Eating & Develop Intuitive Eating Habits to Keep Your Weight Down

Emotional Eating: Overcoming Emotional Eating, Food Addiction and Binge Eating for Good

Eating At Night Time: Sleep Disorders, Health and Hunger Pangs: Tips On What You Can Do About It

Addiction To Food: Proven Help For Overcoming Binge Eating Compulsion And Dependence

Weight Loss: How To Not Gain Holiday Weight After Thanks Giving & Christmas Holidays Beat Post Vacation Weight Gain: Proven Ways To Jumpstart Healthy Eating

Weight Loss After Having A Baby: How To Lose Postpartum Weight After Pregnancy & Giving Birth

Food Addiction And Emotional Eating Guidebook: Proven Ways To End Binge Eating, Sugar Cravings & Eating At Night-Time

Eating Disorders: Food Addiction & Its Effects, What Can You Do If You Can't Stop Overeating?

Slim Down Sensibly: A Realistic Guide to Achieving
Sustainable Weight Loss A Science-Based Approach to
Healthy Eating, Exercise, and Mindset for Lasting Results

Eye Care
Glaucoma Signs And Symptoms

Food Addiction
Overcoming Food Addiction to Sugar, Junk Food. Stop Binge
Eating and Bad Emotional Eating Habits
Food Addiction: Overcoming Emotional Eating, Binge
Eating and Night Eating Syndrome
Weight Loss Without Dieting: 21 Easy Ways To Lose Weight
Naturally
Weight Loss Affirmations For Food Addicts: You Can Do It
Believe In Yourself Daily Positive Affirmations To Help You
Lose Weight

Grief, Bereavement, Death, Loss
Coping with Loss & Dealing with Grief: Surviving
Bereavement, Healing & Recovery After the Death of a Loved
One
How to Plan a Funeral
Coping With Grief And Heartache Of Losing A Pet: Loss Of
A Beloved Furry Companion: Easing The Pain For Those
Affected By Animal Bereavement

Grieving The Loss Of Your Baby: Coping With The Devastation Shock And Heartbreak Of Losing A Child Through Miscarriage, Still Birth

Loss And Grief: Treatment And Discovery Understanding Bereavement, Moving On From Heartbreak And Despair To Recovery

Grief: The Grieving Process, Reactions, Stages Of Grief, Risks, Other Losses And Recovery

First Steps In The Process Of Dealing With Grief: Help for Grieving People: A Guidebook for Coping with Loss. Pain, Heartbreak and Sadness That Won't Go Away

Health Fitness

How To Avoid Colds and Flu Everyday Tips to Prevent or Lessen The Impact of Viruses During Winter Season

Boost Your Immune System Fast: Guide On Proven Ways For Boosting Your Immunity Against Illness And Disease.

International Cooking

Spicy Seafood Dishes: Gourmet Cooking Ideas For Curry And Spice Lovers. Introductory Guide To Decadent Seafood Cuisine With Health Benefits & Wellbeing For The Connoisseur

Noodles: Noodle Recipes Introductory Guide To Delicious Spicy Cuisine International Asian Cooking

50 More Ways to Use Quark Low-fat Soft Cheese: The
Natural Alternative When Cooking Classic Meals
Quark Cheese Recipes: 21 Delicious Breakfast Smoothie
Ideas Using Quark Cheese
30 Healthy Ways to Use Quark Low-fat Soft Cheese
Introduction To Quark Cheese And 25 Recipe Suggestions:
Quark Cheese Guide And Recipes

Quit Alcohol
How To Stop Drinking Alcohol: Coping With Alcoholism,
Signs, Symptoms, Proven Treatment And Recovery

Relationships
The Grief Of Getting Over A Relationship Breakup: How To
Accept Breaking Up With Your Ex | Advice And Tips To
Move On
Coping With A Marriage Breakup: How To Get Over The
Emotional Heartbreak Of A Relationship Breakdown, Signs
Of Splitting Up, Divorce And Heal From A Broken Heart

Self Help
OCD: Introduction Guide Book Obsessive Compulsive
Disorder And How To Recover

Sleep Disorders
Sleep Better at Night and Cure Insomnia Especially When
Stressed

Standalone
Family Style Asian Cookbook: Authentic Eurasian Recipes:
Traditional Anglo-Burmese & Anglo-Indian
Coping with Loss and Dealing with Grief: The Stages of Grief
and 20 Simple Ways on How to Get Through the Bad Days
Coping With Grief Of A Loved One After A Suicide:
Grieving The Devastation And Loss Of Someone Who Took
Their Own Life. How Long Does The Heartache Last?
When A Person Goes Missing And Cannot Be Found:
Coping With The Grief And Devastation, Without Losing
Hope, Of When An Adult Or Child Disappears
Menopause For Women: Signs Symptoms And Treatments A
Simple Guide
Remembering Me: Discover Your Memory Proven Ways To
Expand & Increase It As You Get Older
Boredom: How To Overcome Feeling Bored Discover Over
100 Proven Ways To Beat Apathy
Putting Baby To Sleep: Soothe Your Newborn Baby To Sleep
For Longer Stretches At Night Proven Practical Survival
Guide For Tired Busy New Parents
Coping With Bullying And Cyberbullying: What Parents,
Teachers, Office Managers, And Spouses Need To Know:

How To Identify, Deal With And Cope With A Bully At Home, In School Or In The Workplace

Gardening For Beginners: How To Improve Mental Health, Happiness And Well Being Outdoors In The Garden: Green Finger Holistic Approach In Nature: Everything You Need To Know, Even If You Know Nothing!

Becoming Vegan For Health And The Environment: Plant Based Veganism Guidebook For Beginners: Balanced View Of The Benefits & Risks Of Being Vegetarian

Happiness & Reading Books: For Adults & Children A Proven Way To Increase Literacy Focus Improve Memory Sleep Better Relieve Stress Broaden Your Knowledge Increase Confidence Motivation & Be Happy

Caring For A Loved One With Cancer & Chemotherapy Treatment: An Easy Guide for Caregivers

Genealogy Tracing Your Roots A Comprehensive Guide To Family History Research Uncovering Your Ancestry, Building Your Family Tree And Preserving Your Heritage

Ingram Content Group UK Ltd.
Milton Keynes UK
UKHW010640200723
425492UK00004B/211